Favourite
Songs
You've
Always
Wanted
To Sing

CHESTER MUSIC

(a division of Music Sales Ltd.)

8-9 Frith Street, London, WID 3JB
Exclusive distributors: Music Sales Ltd., Newmarket Road,
Bury St Edmunds, Suffolk, IP33 3YB

Against All Odds
(Take A Look At Me Now)

Words & Music by Phil Collins

1. How can I just let you walk a-way, just let you leave with-out a trace, when I __stand here tak-ing ev-'ry breath with you?__ Ooh,_____ you're the

yeah.

Take_ a look at me now._____ Take_ a look at me now._

Take a look at me now._____

Verse 3:
I wish I could just make you turn around,
Turn around and see me cry.
There's so much I need to say to you,
So many reasons why.
You're the only one
Who really knew me at all.

So take a look at me now,
Well, there's just an empty space.
There's nothing left here to remind me,
Just the memory of your face.
Oh, take a look at me now.
So there's just an empty space.
But to wait for you is all I can do
And that's what I've got to face.

Amazing Grace

Traditional
Arranged by Julian Smith

1. A - ma - zing___ grace! How
(Verses 2 & 3 see block lyric)

sweet the sound that___ saved a___ wretch like___

me.___ I___ once was lost but

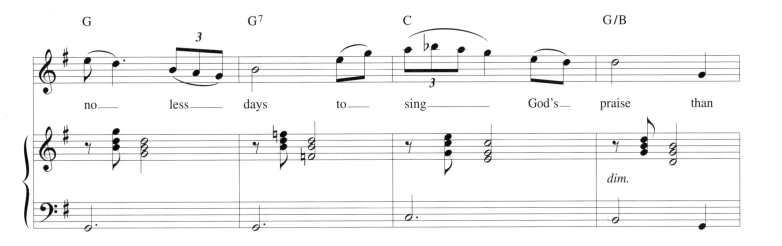

no ——— less ——— days to ——— sing ——— God's ——— praise ——— than

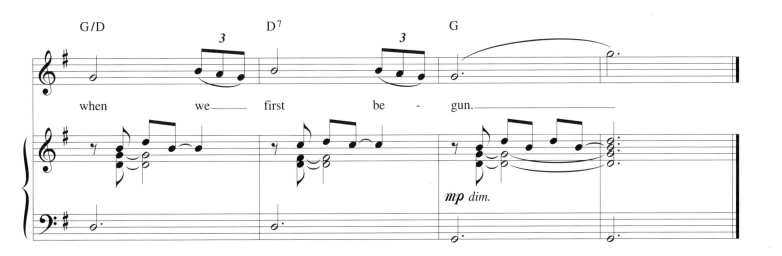

when we ——— first be - gun. ———

Verse 2:
'Twas grace that taught my heart to fear,
And grace my fear relieved.
How precious did that grace appear,
The hour I first believed.

Verse 3:
Through many dangers, toils and snares
We have already come.
'Twas grace that brought us safe thus far,
And grace will lead us home.

Angels

Words & Music by Robbie Williams & Guy Chambers

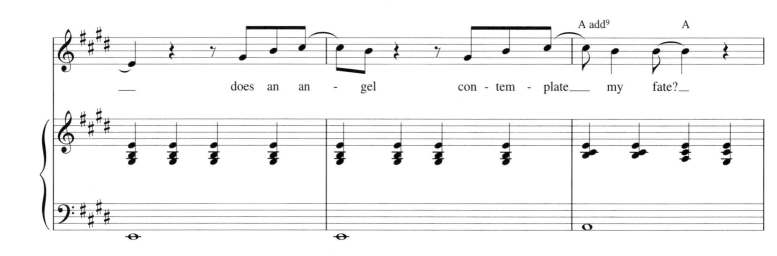

when we're grey and old?___ 'Cause I have been___

told that sal - va - tion lets their wings___ un - fold,___

So when I'm ly - ing in my bed thoughts

run - ning through my head and I feel that love is dead,___

As Long As He Needs Me

(From "Oliver")
Words & Music by Lionel Bart

Moderately

He does-n't act as tho' he cares, but deep in-side I know he cares, and this is why, I'm tied right by his side.

As long as he needs me____ I know where I must be.____ I'll cling on stead - fast - ly,____ as long as he needs me.____ As long as life is long,____ I'll love him, right or wrong;____ and some - how I'll be strong,____ as long as

Auld Lang Syne

Traditional

Auld_____ Lang_____ Syne. We'll tak' a cup o'

kind - ness yet, for___ Auld_____ Lang_____ Syne.

Verse 2:
We twa ha'e run about the braes,
And pu'd the gowans fine;
But we've wander'd mony a weary foot,
Sin Auld Lang Syne.
Chorus

Verse 3:
We twa ha'e sported i' the burn,
Frae mornin' sun 'til dine,
But seas between us braid ha'e roared,
Sin Auld Lang Syne.
Chorus

Verse 4:
And here's a hand my trusty friend,
And gie's a hand o' thine,
We'll tak' a cup o' kindness yet,
For Auld Lang Syne.
Chorus

Born To Be Wild

Words & Music by Mars Bonfire

1. Get your mo-tor run - ning,— head out on the high - way,

(Verses 2 & 3 see block lyric)

look-ing for ad-ven - ture, in what -

Verse 2:
I like smoke and lightning,
Heavy metal thunder,
Racing in the wind,
And the feeling that I'm under.

Yeah darlin' *etc.*

Verse 3: (𝄋.) — as Verse 1

Big Spender

(From "Sweet Charity")
Music by Cy Coleman
Words by Dorothy Fields

I don't pop my cork for ev'-ry guy I see.

Hey! Big Spen-der,— Spend a lit-tle time— with

me. Would-n't you like to have

fun, fun, fun? How's a-bout a few laughs, laughs? I can show you a

good time,___ Let me show you a___ good time.___ The min-ute you

Can't Help Falling In Love

Words & Music by George David Weiss, Hugo Peretti & Luigi Creatore

Crazy

Words & Music by Willie Nelson

Don't Know Why

Words & Music by Jesse Harris

Verse 3:
Out across the endless sea
I will die in ecstasy
But I'll be a bag of bones
Driving down the road alone.

My heart is drenched in wine etc.

Verse 4:
Something has to make you run
I don't know why I didn't come
I feel as empty as a drum
I don't know why I didn't come
I don't know why I didn't come
I don't know why I didn't come

Down By The Riverside

Traditional

riv - er - side, down by the riv - er - side._____ Then I'll

take her lit - tle hand, just so she will un - der - stand

what I have got to say._____ I'm gon - na

Don't Look Back In Anger

Words & Music by Noel Gallagher

1. Slip in - side___ the eye of your mind,___ don't you know you might___ find___
(Verse 2 see block lyric)

a bet - ter place to play.___

Verse 2:
Take me to the place where you go,
Where nobody knows if it's night or day.
Please don't put your life in the hands
Of a rock 'n' roll band who'll throw it all away.

I'm gonna start a revolution from my bed.
'Cause you said the brains I had went to my head.
Step outside, the summertime's in bloom.
Stand up beside the fireplace, take that look from off your face,
'Cause you ain't never gonna burn my heart out.

Evergreen

Words & Music by Jørgen Elofsson, Per Magnusson & David Kreuger

Verse 2:
Touch like an angel,
Like velvet to my skin,
And I wonder,
I wonder why you wanna stay the night,
What you're dreaming,
What's behind.
Don't tell me, but it feels like love.

I'm gonna take this moment *etc.*

Eternal Flame

Words & Music by Billy Steinberg, Tom Kelly & Susanna Hoffs

Hopelessly Devoted To You

(From "Grease")
Words & Music by John Farrar

-vot-ed_____ to you._____

D.%. al Coda

3. My

⊕ Coda

-vot-ed_____ to

you._____

Verse 2:
I know I'm just a fool who's willin'
To sit around and wait for you.
But, baby, can't you see
There's nothin' else for me to do.

Verse 3:
My head is sayin' "Fool, forget him."
My heart is sayin' "Don't let go.
Hold on to the end."
And that's what I intend to do.

I'm Called Little Buttercup

(From "HMS Pinafore")
Music by Sir Arthur Sullivan
Words by W. S. Gilbert

still I'm called But - ter - cup, poor Lit - tle But - ter - cup, sweet Lit - tle But - ter - cup I! I've snuff and to - bac - cy, and ex - cel - lent jac - ky, I've scis - sors, and watch - es and knives; I've rib - bons and la - ces to set off the fa - ces of pret - ty young sweet - hearts and wives. I've

trea - cle and tof - fee, I've tea and I've cof - fee, soft

tom - my and suc - cu - lent chops; I've chick - ens and

rall.

co - nies, and pret - ty po - lo - nies, and ex - cel - lent pep - per - mint

a tempo

drops.＿＿＿＿＿ Then buy of your But - ter - cup, dear Lit - tle

But - ter - cup, Sai - lors should nev - er be shy; So

buy of your But - ter - cup, poor Lit - tle But - ter - cup, come, of your

But - ter - cup buy.____

colla voce

f

Is You Is Or Is You Ain't My Baby?

(From "Five Guys Named Moe")
Words & Music by Billy Austin & Louis Jordan

I got-ta girl who's al-ways late, an-y-time we have a date but I love her,_____ yes I love her._____

Luck Be A Lady

(From "Guys And Dolls")
Words & Music by Frank Loesser

I know they say you've treat-ed oth-er guys you've been with. Luck be a
la-dy with me.
la-dy does-n't leave her es-cort. It is-n't
fair, it is-n't nice! A

Londonderry Air

Traditional

Slowly

Would God I were the ten-der ap-ple blos-som ___ that floats and falls from off the twist-ed bough, ___ to lie and faint with-in your silk-en bo-som, with-in your silk-en bo - - som, as that does

Light My Fire

Words & Music by Jim Morrison, Robbie Krieger, Ray Manzarek & John Densmore

1. You know that it would be un-true,___ you know that I would be a li-
(Verses 2 & 3 see block lyric)

Oh,_____ come_____ on ba - by light__ my___ fire.

Come on ba - by light,_____ light my fire.__ Light my fire,__ light my fire,__ light my fire.__

Repeat ad lib. to fade

_____ Oh,__ yeah.__ Light it, light__ it, light it, light it, light it, light__ it, yes,__ girl.__ Ooh.

Verse 2:
The time to hesitate is through
There's no time to wallow in the mire
If I was to say to you
That our love becomes a funeral pyre.

Come on baby, light my fire   *etc.*

Verse 3:
The time to hesitate is through
There's no time to wallow in the mire
Try now we can only lose
And our love becomes a funeral pyre.

Come on baby, light my fire   *etc.*

Moon River

(From "Breakfast At Tiffany's")
Music by Henry Mancini
Words by Johnny Mercer

My Bonnie Lies Over The Ocean

Traditional

Verse 2:
Oh, blow ye winds over the ocean,
And blow ye winds over the sea,
Oh, blow ye winds over the ocean,
And bring back my Bonnie to me.
Chorus

Verse 3:
Last night, as I lay on my pillow,
Last night, as I lay on my bed,
Last night as I lay on my pillow,
I dreamed my poor Bonnie was dead.
Chorus

Verse 4:
The winds have blown over the ocean,
The winds have blown over the sea,
The winds have blown over the ocean,
And brought my Bonnie to me.
Chorus

Perfect Moment

Words & Music by James Marr & Wendy Page

1. This is my mo - ment, this is my per - fect mo - ment with you. This is what

Sail Away

Words & Music by David Gray

Sail a-way— with me, ho-ney, I put my heart— in your hands.

Sail a-way— with me ho-ney now,— now,— now.—

and ev - 'ry - thing I held so dear

dis - ap - peared with - out a trace.

1. Though all the times I tast - ed love,
(Verse 2 see block lyric)

nev - er knew quite what I had.

Lit - tle dar - ling, if you hear me now,

nev - er need - ed you so bad;

spin - ning 'round in - side my head.

Sail a - way with me, ho - ney, I put my heart in your hands.

99

Verse 2:
I've been talking drunken gibberish,
Falling in and out of bars.
Trying to get some explanation here,
For the way some people are.
How did it ever come so far?

Chorus 5:
Sail away with me, honey,
I put my heart in your hands.
It break me up if you put me down, woh…
Sail away with me; what will be will be.
I wanna hold you now, now, now.

Chorus 6 & 7:
(Whistle)

Swing Low, Sweet Chariot

Traditional

Something

Words & Music by George Harrison

Verse 3:
Something in the way she knows,
And all I have to do is think of her.
Something in the things she shows me,
I don't want to leave her now,
You know I believe and how.

When All Night A Chap Remains

(From "Iolanthe")
Music by Sir Arthur Sullivan
Words by W. S. Gilbert

1. When

all night long a chap re - mains on sen - try go, to chase mo-
in that House M. P.'s di - vide, if they've a brain and ce - re -

accel. poco a poco

109

rall.　　　　　　　　　　Tempo Iº ♩ = 69

-ton - ish you.　　　I　of - ten think it's com - i - cal—
-nim - i - ty.　　　Then　let's re - joice with loud Fal, lal—

Fal, lal,＿ la!　Fal, lal,＿ la!　How
Fal, lal,＿ la!　Fal, lal,＿ la!　That

na - ture al - ways

does con - trive—　Fal, lal,＿ la,＿ la!　That＿ ev - 'ry boy and＿

ev - 'ry gal that's born in - to the＿ world a - live　Is

either a lit-tle Lib-er-al or else a lit-tle Con-ser-va-tive!

Fal, lal,___ la! Fal, lal,___ la! Is ei-ther a lit-tle Lib-er-al or

else a lit-tle Con-ser-va-tive! Fal, lal, la!

2. When

Your Song

Words & Music by Elton John & Bernie Taupin

Slow, but with a beat

1. It's a lit-tle bit fun-ny_____ this feel-ing in-side,_____
(Verses 2, 3 & 4 see block lyric)

I'm not one of those___ who__ can eas-i-ly hide,_____

I don't have much mon - ey_ but, boy, if I did,_

I'd buy_ a big house where__ we both_ could live.

this one's_ for you._

And you_ can tell ev - 'ry - bo - dy This_ is your song._____

Last time to Coda

It may_ be quite sim-ple but,___ now that it's done,___

I hope you don't mind,___ I hope you don't mind___ that I put_ down in_ words. How

rit.   **a tempo**   *D.S. (with repeat) al Coda*

won-der-ful life is___ while you're in___ the world.

Coda

I hope you don't mind,___ I hope you don't mind___ that I put_ down in_ words, How

114

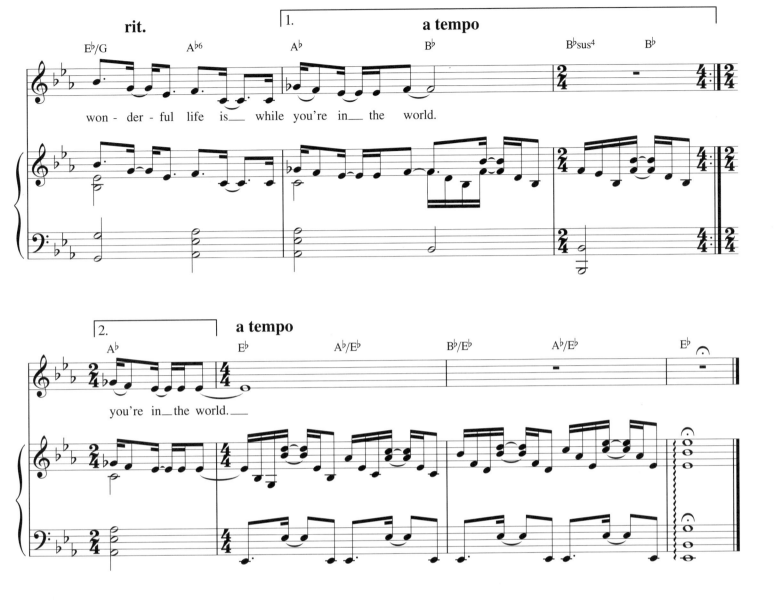

Verse 2:
If I was a sculptor but then again no,
Or a man who makes potions in a travelin' show,
I know it's not much but it's the best I can do,
My gift is my song and this one's for you.

Chorus:
And you can tell ev'rybody this is your song.
It may be quite simple but, now that it's done,
I hope you don't mind, I hope you don't mind that I put down in words
How wonderful life is while you're in the world.

Verse 3:
I sat on the roof and kicked off the moss,
Well a few of the verses, well they've got me quite cross,
But the sun's been quite kind while I wrote this song,
It's for people like you, that keep it turned on.

Verse 4:
So excuse me forgetting but these things I do,
You see I've forgotten if they're green or they're blue.
Anyway the thing is what I really mean,
Yours are the sweetest eyes I've ever seen.

Chorus:
And you can tell ev'rybody *etc.*

You're Still The One

Words & Music by Shania Twain & R. J. Lange

Verse 2:
Ain't nothing better,
We beat the odds together,
I'm glad we didn't listen,
Look at what we would be missing.

They said, I bet,
They'll never make it,
But just look at us holding on,
We're still together, still going strong.

The Scientist

Words & Music by Guy Berryman, Jon Buckland,
Will Champion & Chris Martin

1. Come up to meet__ you, tell you I'm sor - ry, you don't know how love-
(Verse 2 see block lyric)

Verse 2:
I was just guessing at numbers and figures,
Pulling the puzzles apart.
Questions of science, science and progress
Do not speak as loud as my heart.
Tell me you love me, and come back and haunt me,
Oh, when I rush to the start.
Running in circles, chasing tails,
Comin' a-back as we are.

Nobody said it was easy *etc.*

Yesterday

Words & Music by John Lennon & Paul McCartney

Moderately, with expression

1. Yes - ter - day, _____ all my trou - bles seemed so
2. Sud - den - ly, _____ I'm not half the man _____ I

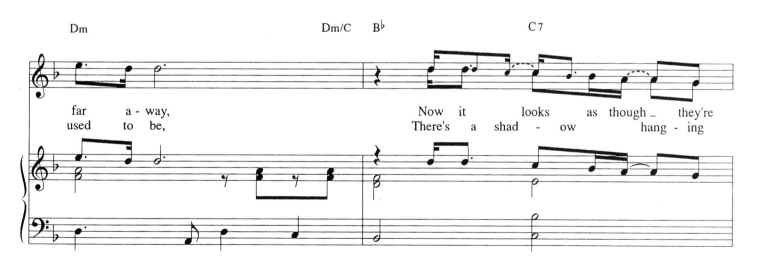

far a - way, Now it looks as though _____ they're
used to be, There's a shad - ow hang - ing

If you like this book you will also like these...